Latin Made Simple Through Stories

Volumen Duo

EASY LATIN

CONTENTS

INTRODUCTION

This book was created in conjunction with the Easy Latin Youtube channel found here (where you can find audio lessons):

https://youtube.com/c/EasyLatin

    The most effective way to learn a language is in context, because not only is it easier to learn new words this way, but you will also acquire grammar organically. And it's much more fun and interesting to learn this way than to memorize grammar tables. In these book, we will be learning directly from simple sentences in Latin and you may be surprised how easily and quickly you will acquire this beautiful language.   Let's go!

LESSON 16

Salvēte omnēs!   Hi everybody!

We still have a long way to go with the past tense, so let's begin with a little review.
Do you remember Julius Caeser's famous phrase?

Venī, vidī, vīcī   I came, I saw, I conquered.

These are all in perfect past tense. We can use the phrase to remember the first-person case for this tense. Try to say now, I came here.

Hīc venī.   And how do we say I drank wine.

Vīnum bibī.   This one's a little harder, but can you remember how to say, He saw pebbles?

Calculōs vīdit.   Remember we imagined little pebbles or calculus being scraped off our teeth.

There is another pattern we have to learn which the ARE verbs use. This is AV plus the perfect ending.

In Ītaliā habitāvī.   I lived in Italy.

You see, we add a long A and V, then the appropriate ending.

Try to say now, He or she walked to the forest.

Ad silvam ambulāvit.

Regular ARE verbs all use AV plus the appropriate ending, so it's a good one to remember. For IRE verbs, there is a similar conjugation:

Nimis dormīvī.   I overslept.

Remember this word Nimis? It means too much, so this literally means, I slept too much. So, similar to the ARE conjugation, this IRE verb added a long I and V plus the appropriate ending. Unfortunately there are other patterns that other IRE verbs also use.

There are so many different forms that it's easy to get overwhelmed, so let's move on to something else for now.

Can you remember back to the first lesson the phrase meaning, "He who teaches, learns."

Quī docet, discit.

Try to figure out now what the next sentence means:

Amīcum habeo, quī Romae habitat.

I have a friend who lives in Rome.

Notice that WHO, refers to the friend. So as you can probably guess, it has to match gender. Quī is the masculine form. We saw a similar line in the beginning of Pater Noster:

Pater noster, quī es in caelīs,

For feminine nouns, we switch it to quae.
Try to say now, I have a daughter who is a teacher.

Fīliam habeo, quae magistra est.

These words function grammatically exactly like their English counterparts as you can see in the next sentence.

Puella, quae scrībit, soror mea est.

The girl, who is writing, is my sister.   And try to say now, the boy, who is reading, is my brother.
Puer, quī legit, frater meus est.

In Latin some verbs are reflexive verbs, which we don't really have in English. I mentioned this in the story of Europa in Lesson 3, because this was used when Jupiter changed into a bull. We had the sentence:

Iūppiter sē in taurum trānsfōrmat.

This small word sē is like saying himself, but in reality, it indicates that the subject and object are the same. In other words, it reflects the action back on the subject. But it's similar to saying that Jupiter transformed himself into a bull.

But this word sē can also mean each other as in the next sentence.

Parentēs meī inter sē amābant.   My parents loved each other.

The word INTER just means between or among.

In the story, we will see the following:

Syringa sē in silvā occultābat.

Syringa is the name of a character in the story.

We actually have the verb occult in English, meaning to cut off from view, but it's not very commonly used. In Latin this word means to hide, just like how secret societies that are involved in the occult are hidden. So in this sentence, Syringa sē occultābat means Syringa hid herself. The imperfect is used because the action extends up until another action interrupts it.

Continuing with the imperfect, try to say, The father, who lived in the forest.

Pater, quī in silvā habitābat.   And look at the next sentence.

Tē amābam.   I loved you.

In English, the first- and third-person pronouns still have different forms, me, him, her, but we no longer use thee in modern English. If you've read a lot of Shakespeare, you can make the association between Tē amō and I love thee.

Can you guess which pronoun is in the next sentence?

Eam amābat.

He loved her. Or she loved her. Depending on the context. And from this word, can you guess what the male version is? Try to say, I saw him.

Eum vidī.

Can you guess what the next sentence means?

Nihil dīxit.   He or she said nothing.

For this lesson's story, we need to have a little background from Greek mythology. Nymphs were fantasy creatures that lived in rivers who had magical powers. They weren't goddesses, but more like personifications of nature although they were depicted as beautiful maidens. The story also features Pan, the Greek god with horns and whose lower body looked like a goat's legs. He was a god of the wild and rustic music.

Pān et Syringa

Ōlim erat nympha pulchra, quae nōmen Syringa erat. Omnēs deī Syringam amābant, sed Syringa deōs nōn amābat. Syringa deōs fugitābat et sē in silvā occultābat.
Deus Pān, quī in silvā habitābat, Syringam vīdit et eam amābat. Pān dīxit, "Tē amō."

Pan and Syrinx

Once upon a time, there was a beautiful nymph whose name was Syrinx.
All the gods loved Syrinx, but Syrinx did not love the gods. Syrinx fled from the gods and hid herself in the forest.
The god Pan, who lived in the forest, saw Syrinx and loved her. Pan said, "I love you."

I expect that you were able to guess the meaning of any new words, but just to clarify: Omnēs deī means Every god, or all the gods. And deōs is the plural accusative form of Deus. Okay, we'll finish this story in the next lesson.

LESSON 17

We learned two new forms for the perfect past tense that were very similar in the last lesson. Say, the farmer worked.

Agricola labōrāvit.   Now say, I didn't sleep.

Nōn dormīvī.

These two forms are very similar, because it's like we keep the long vowel at the end and add V. And, recalling Julius Caesar's famous phrase, say now, I saw a male friend.

Amīcum vidī.   And how did we say, He or she said nothing.

Nihil dīxit.   This lesson's story contains all ARE verbs, except one, so we will stick to just practicing these forms for now.
Can you figure out the next sentence?

Miser et īnfēlīx eram. Or, for females. Misera et īnfēlīx eram.   I was miserable and unhappy. We saw the word fēlīx earlier and the prefix IN is the Latin equivalent to UN and NON. We also have this prefix in certain words derived from Latin like Infinite, or not finite. And miser obviously means miserable and also pitiful, wretched, etc. Note also, miser declines according to gender, but īnfēlīx does not.

One word for river is fluvius. We can remember this word by thinking that water is fluving down the river. This also has roots in fluent and flux, because when we speak fluently, we speak fluidly. Look at the next sentence now. She or he fled to the river.

Nympha ad fluvium fugitāvit.   The nymph fled to the river.

We will see this phrase in the story. Another phrase in the story is this one:

Ō nymphae! Fōrmam meam mūtāte!

Oh nymphs! Change my form!

This is a good sentence for review. Here Ō nymphae is the vocative form, which is usually the same as the nominative form, but is used to address someone. Fōrma is obvious and then we have mūtāte. Can you tell what form this is? It's the imperative plural form. Just like Salvēte it has a te on the end to indicate it's the plural and the imperative is normally just the dictionary form of the verb minus RE. Let's try some other words in imperative form. Say to one person, Work!

Labōrā!   Now, Read the book!

Librum lege.   And what does this mean?

Fac iterum.   Do it again.

Try to say now, to multiple people, Say that again.

Dīcite iterum.

After Syringa tells the nymphs to change her form, we have the sentence:

Deinde nymphae eam in pap□ rōs in fluviō mūtāvit.

We saw eam in the last lesson, remember? It means her. And the word pap□ rus can refer to the paper, garment, or plant that the first two are made from. Here it is the plant, the paper reed.

And we also have two uses of IN in this sentence. Can you see the difference? in pap□ rōs is the object, but it's plural, so this is what she is turned into.

And   in fluviō is the location, which we can tell because it's the ablative. So this sentence means:

Then the nymphs changed her into paper reeds in the river. And from EAM can you guess what the male plural version is?

Eōs

So this means THEM, when referring to something masculine like pap□rōs.
Try to guess the next sentence:

Septem pap□rōs adhaesit.   He or she attaches seven reeds.

Can you see the connection to adhesive. It's clearer in the written form. And
the present tense is:

adhaeret   which resembles adhere But we can see that this is an irregular
verb, since the r changes to S in the past tense.   The story ends with this
sentence:

Dēnique septem pap□rōs adhaesit et fistulam fōrmāvit.

If you recall, the words Prīmō   Deinde   Dēnique   are used to narrate a
sequence of events. They are roughly equivalent to first, then, and finally.
Fōrmāvit obviously means formed. We also just saw Forma, which was the
noun meaning form. In Latin, there are two different forms for form, but in
English we only have form. English is weird like that. And then the word
fistula can mean things like a tube or a pipe and also refers to the pipes of
Pan.

This is the story of the origin of the Pan flute, which looks like this:
It usually has seven or more pipes of varying length that were played by
blowing air over the openings.
Okay, let's finish the story of:

Pān et Syringa.

    Sed nympha misera ad fluvium fugitāvit. Syringa ad nymphās clāmāvit,
"Ō nymphae! Fōrmam meam mūtāte!" Deinde nymphae eam in pap□rōs in
fluviō mūtāvit. Pān pap□rōs vīdit et eōs amābat. Dēnique septem pap□rōs
adhaesit et fistulam fōrmāvit.

Pan and Syrinx

    But the miserable nymph fled to the river. Syrinx cried to the nymphs,
"Oh nymphs! Change my form!"
    Then the nymphs changed her into paper reeds in the river. Pan saw the
reeds and loved them.

Finally, he attached seven reeds and formed a fistula.

We still have a ways to go with the past tense, but hopefully you're starting to be able to recognize the forms when you read and remember some of the endings like āvī and āvit. Try to also pay attention to when the imperfect tense is being used and to figure out why it is being used instead of the perfect tense. Remember, the perfect tense is used for completed actions. Brief actions that were done once, not acts that were continuous or habitual. These are covered by the imperfect tense, which is also used for descriptions in a narrative like, "The house was big." But don't worry if you don't remember all this, we will obviously be seeing much more of the past tense in the stories to come.

LESSON 18

In this lesson we will begin with the story and explain it along the way just like in Lesson 13 with Maximus et Valentina. But before we start, can you recall the word for river?

Fluvius

Let's go!

Videsne fluvius? Nīlus est. Hic fluvius vēlōciter fluit. Multī piscēs in fluviō natant.

Hopefully you understood most of the words in these sentences. The Nile is Nīlus in Latin. And vēlōciter is an adjective meaning rapidly, swiftly. The astrological sign Pisces can help you remember the word for fish in Latin, because they are spelled the same.

We actually have the word natant in English, but it's an adjective meaning swimming or floating.

Natant kind of reminds me of the word nautical, so it seems to have something to do with water. And as you may have guessed, this verb means to swim.

Fluvius

Ubi est Nīlus? Nīlus nōn in Eurōpā est. In Āfricā est.
Mississippiensis quoque fluvius est. Sed Mississippiensis nōn in Āfricā est. In Americā est.

Quam longus est fluvius Nīlus? Nīlus est fluvius longissimus mundī.
I'm sure you understood these sentences, but let's break them down a little.
Quam means how much, or to what degree and it can be used in exclamations
like the following:

Quam horribile!   How horrible!   And

Quam pulchram est!   How beautiful she is!

To remember the word mundus, think of the phrase mundane world. Here
mundī is the genitive or possessive form, so it's saying The Nile is the world's
longest river.

-issim_ is like the ending -EST in English. It has the meaning of "the
most...whatever" But because this is Latin, the ending -issim has to decline
like an adjective. For example:

Epistula logissima mundī est.   It is the world's longest letter.

Okay, that's enough about rivers, let's move on to cities now. One word for
city is urbs. This is where we get the word urban. It is a feminine word,
which you might be able to remember because in English it's URBAn. Let's
continue.

Rōma urbs antīqua est. Haec urbs in Ītaliā est. Urbs historica est.

Estne Rōma urbs magna? Habitasne in urbē? Bibliothēca in urbē est.

Did you understand the word antīqua? It sounds a lot like antique, but has a
meaning more like ancient. So this sentence means Rome is an ancient city.
And remember haec is the feminine form of hic.

Then we have two questions: remember Yes/no questions add the suffix NE
to the first word. And the last sentence contains the word Bibliothēca. This
is a place where bibliophiles can go to make a bibliography. A library. In
Latin, the word Librāria refers to a female bookseller. If you speak a romance
language, this might be familiar. Try to say now, The male student is reading
in the library.

Discipulus in bibliothēcā legit.

Let's use this word a little more now.

Multī librī in bibliothēcā sunt. Bibliothēca in mediā urbē est. Ubi est schola tua? Schola iūxtā bibliothēcam est.

The first sentence here means There are many books in the library. And the following sentence says that The library is in the middle of the city. Note, both mediā and urbē are in the ablative form because the city is the location and mediā is an adjective modifying urbē, so it has to match form.

In the final sentence, we see the preposition iūxtā plus the accusative form. The forms that the words take after prepositions in Latin doesn't always make sense, but the best way to learn them is through repetition by making up your own example sentences.

Let's try a few sentences using this preposition before we end.

Try to say, There is a river beside the house.

Fluvius iūxtā domum est.

And how about, I am next to Maximus.

Iūxtā Maximum sum.

Finally, here is the name of two European countries in Latin, can you guess which they are?

Gallia iūxtā Hispāniam est.

Gaul, (or modern day France and Belgium) and Hispania (or modern day Spain   and   Portugal).

LESSON 19

Let's review the new words we learned: How did we say, There are many books in the library.

Multī librī in bibliothēcā sunt.

Now try, There is a library in the city.

Bibliothēca in urbē est.

And can you remember how to say, The school is next to the library.

Schola iūxtā bibliothēcam est.

In each of these sentences, Bibliothēca has a different ending. Don't worry if you didn't get all of them right. It takes a long time to acquire these aspects of grammar. It's more important that you notice any errors you make and then figure out why each one is used so you can correct yourself.

So here in the first sentence, Bibliothēca is in the ablative form because it indicates a location. In the second it is the subject (and urbs is in the ablative). And in the third sentence, it is in the accusative, simply because the preposition iūxtā requires it. Let's try something a little easier now.

Minerva is the Roman name for Athena, so try to say, Minerva was a goddess.

Minerva dea erat.

And look at the next sentence now.

Erat dea artium.

She was goddess of the arts.

Notice that we have the ending IUM here. This is the plural genitive form of third-declension nouns. But don't try to memorize the ending. Learn the chunk "dea artium" and associate it with goddess of the arts. Because remember, we don't learn language through grammar, we learn grammar through language. When we learn enough chunks like this, the grammar comes naturally. Another similar chunk comes in the last two words of the next sentence.

Erat perīta in artibus.

Perīta means skilled. If you do something PERfectly, you must be really skilled. Also PERIcles was a very skilled ruler of Athens.

And the chunk "in artibus" contains -IBUS, the ablative plural ending for third-declension nouns.

You might see in artibus in the following phrase on a degree for universities that like to be fancy.

Baccalaureus in artibus

This means Bachelor in the arts. Or a Bachelor's degree in liberal arts.

Bacca is Latin for berry, and laurea means laurels, so this referred to the fact that graduates would wear laurel crowns filled with berries that represented the fruits of their study.

Have you heard the Spanish phrase, Mi casa es tu casa? This is equivalent to saying, Make yourself at home, but the literal meaning is My house is your house. Latin also uses the word casa for house, but it sometimes refers to a hut or cabin in classical Latin. We also learned another word for house, can you remember what it was?

Domus   And this is a weird noun because it is actually feminine even though it looks masculine.

However, casa is a regular first-declension noun. So, this sentence means? The first word is a name.

Arachnē in casā minūtā habitābat.

Arachne lived in a tiny cottage.
Remember, here the imperfect tense is used because the action is incomplete.
And can you guess what the following means?

Arachnē pictūrās pulchrās fōrmāvit.

Arachne formed beautiful pictures.

And in the next sentence, we will have the following word:

Saepe

If you drink something in sips, you have to Saep et (sip it) often, right?

The following sentence is long, but is review. The subject of the second half
is Arachne.

Dum nymphae spectābant, saepe pictūrās in textilī fōrmāvit.

While the nymphs were watching, she often fashioned pictures in textile.

Let's practice the new words we learned. Say, He or she often walks in the
city.

Saepe in urbē ambulat.

Remember, even if you said In Urbs, don't worry so much. The grammar will
come in time. The most important part is expanding your vocabulary. And
how would we say, I often drink in a tiny cottage.

Saepe in casā minūtā bibō.

Can you guess the meaning of the next sentence?

Quis est magistra tibī?

Who is your teacher? But notice, tibī is the dative form of tu.

So it's like saying, Teacher to you. So WHO is Quis in Latin. And What is
very similar. WhaD is it?

Quid   So, using the previous sentence as an example, say now, What is
your name.

Quid est nōmen tibī?
Another common phrase that uses this word is the following:

Grātiās tibī agō.

I give thanks to you.
The word agō means act, do, and a million other things.

You can also just say Grātiās, although this is obviously less formal. Look at
the next sentence now:

Tibī librum dedit.

Dedit is the perfect past tense of dat, which is a highly irregular verb. So this
sentence means He gave the book to you. We will see this word at the very
end of the story.

Okay, we're ready now for the first part of the story of Arachne; however,
there will be one word that I'm sure you can guess.

Arachnē

Minerva dea erat. Erat dea artium. Arachnē erat puella quoque perīta in
artibus.   Arachnē in casā minūtā habitābat et pictūrās pulchrās fōrmāvit.
Dum nymphae spectābant, saepe pictūrās in textilī fōrmāvit.
    Nymphae pictūrās vīdit et puellam laudāvit. "Quis est magistra tibī? Certē
Minerva tibī artem dedit."

Minerva was a goddess. She was goddess of the arts. Arachne was a girl also
skilled in the arts. Arachne lived in a tiny cottage and formed beautiful
pictures. While the nymphs were watching, she often fashioned pictures in
textile.
    The nymphs looked at the pictures and praised the girl. "Who is your
teacher? Certainly Minerva gave you your art."

Did you understand the last sentence?   Certē sounds a lot like Certainly,
right? So this sentence means, "Certainly Minerva gave you your art."
Notice, words like your and my and often left unstated in Latin if their

obvious from context.

LESSON 20

Can you remember the word for often?

Saepe

Remember, If you drink something in sips, you have to Saep et often, right? Say now, I often walk in the city.

Saepe in urbē ambulat.

We learned this word many lessons ago, but can you remember how to say rarely?

Rārō

So this is the opposite of saepe. Say now, I rarely drink in the forest.

Rārō in silvā bibō.

In the last story, we learned how to ask, Who is your teacher? Remember it was worded like Teacher to you. What was it?

Quis est magistra tibī?

Let's answer this by saying, "No one is my teacher."

Nēmō magistra mihī est.

Here we have the dative form of Ego.

And note, tibī and mihī are sometimes written with the macron over and sometimes not. I think it's easier to pronounce with the macron, but you can decide how you want to say it.

The story continued in this lesson is based on a story from Ovid's Metamorphoses. Many stories from this book deal with pride, as well as this one as we'll see. First, the word proud in Latin is:

Superbus   When you do something superbly, you become proud. So how would we say, The girl was proud.

Puella superba erat.

And do you remember how to say, She formed a beautiful picture?

Pictūram pulchram fōrmāvit.

This form of the past tense had āvi and there was another similar ending. Remember, to go is īre. So, She went, would be.

Īvit.   Look at this sentence now.

Dea Minerva fōrmam fēminae simulāvit et ad terram īvit.

Here fōrmam fēminae means feminine form, but note that fēminae is genitive form, so this is more like woman's form. And simulāvit means.... simulate, or make like. Easy right? So altogether: the Goddess Minerva simulated feminine form and went to the earth. This sentence contains two of the most common perfect past tense conjugations. Another common one uses UI. First, can you remember how to say, He teaches the Latin Language.

Linguam Latīnam docet.   And look at this now.

Mē docuī.

I taught myself. You see, to conjugate this past tense form, we remove the ERE, add U and the appropriate ending.

So for the perfect past tense there are three "easy" conjugations:

-āvī
-īvī
-uī

And there are many other less regular conjugations, which are too numerous to sit down and memorize. This is why it is much easier to learn the endings simply through comprehensible input. When we read and hear the endings over and over again, they will come naturally to our tongues, because any other way the words will sound wrong to us. So let's practice this new ending some more.

Bonum magistrum habuī.

I had a good teacher. And in the story we'll see:

Arachnē sapientiam nōn habuit.

Arachne didn't have wisdom. Or, Arachne wasn't wise.

We have the word sapient in English, which also means wise. And this is where we get the word Homo sapiens, or in Latin, Homō sapiēns which means Wise man. And note, we have both the adjective sapiēns   and sapientia.

This IA ending is added to adjectives and some other word types to make them into nouns. Another such pair is

superba and superbia   proud and pride

This second word is contained in the phrase:

Contrītium praecēdit superbia.

Pride goeth before a fall. Or literally, Contrition precedes pride. This will be in the story.

And one final word for this lesson's story.

Certāmus!   Let's compete!

Do you remember in the last lesson, we saw the word Certē, meaning certainly? Both of these words are related to the word certus, meaning something like certain, settled, resolved. So maybe you can see the connection to Certāmus meaning things like compete and fight because you have to settle or resolve a dispute.

And can you remember how to say, With honors. As in Graduated with honors.

Cum laude

And what form is laude?   That's right, Ablative. Cum always triggers the ablative.

Let's try to say now, I often fight with my brother. We haven't seen this yet, but try to guess how we add an E to the word for brother.

Cum frātre saepe certō.   The word frāter loses the E when it declines.

We're now ready for the story, but there is one phrase you need to try to guess first. It's the last thing that Arachne says, which will obviously get her in trouble.

Sed Arachnē superba erat et sapientiam nōn habuit. Sē laudāvit et clāmāvit, "Minerva nōn mē docuit. Nēmō mihi magistra est. Mē docuī. Fōrmō pictūrās melius quam Minerva."
     Dea Minerva fōrmam fēminae simulāvit et ad terram īvit. Dīxit ad puellam, "Contrītium praecēdit superbia. Certāmus!"

But Arachne was proud and was not wise (did not have wisdom). She praised herself and cried, "Minerva did not teach me. No one is my teacher. I taught myself. I form pictures better than Minerva."
     The goddess Minerva simulated feminine form and went to the earth. She said to the girl, "Pride goeth before a fall. (Contrition precedes pride.) Let's compete!"

Did you guess that Fōrmō pictūrās melius quam Minerva. Means, I form pictures better than Minerva. Melius quam is another important chunk we should learn. We'll see this more in the next lesson.

And did you understand Sē laudāvit? It means she praised herself.

Okay, in the next lesson we'll finish this story and find out what's up with the name Arachne.

LESSON 21

Let's briefly review the three easy conjugations of the perfect past tense. Remember, these refer to actions completed in the past.
Say, I worked in Italy.

In Ītaliā labōrāvī.   And now, I went to school.

Ad scholam īvī.

Bonum magistrum habuī.   I had a good teacher.

And do you remember the two words that meant "better than"?

Melius quam   Look at the next sentence:

Valentina melius quam Maximus natāre potest.

Valentina can swim better than Maximus.

Try to say now, I can read better than you.

Ego melius quam tū legere possum.

And try to guess the last word in the next sentence.

Hic liber est melius quam iste.   This book is better than that one.

We use Hic and Haec to refer to things near us and iste and ista to refer to things near the listener, similar to this and that, but a little different as we'll see later. Concentrating on the genders, try to say now, That letter isn't mine.

Ista epistula nōn mea est.   Look at the next sentence now.

Istum librum legere volō.

As you'd expect, these words have to decline, similar to adjectives.

Using the imperfect tense, Try to say now, I was writing that letter.

Istam epistulam scrībēbam.

And these words can actually be used by themselves. For example,

Estne hic gladius tuus? Iste nōn meus est.

Is this your sword? That is not mine.

So as you can see, iste stands alone in the reply, but refers back to the sword. And notice, the first speaker uses hic because the sword is near him or her. And the person who replies uses iste because the sword is near the first speaker.

The next sentence contains a small but really useful word. And if you speak Spanish or French, you'll be able to understand this.

Dē tē cogitō.   I'm thinking of you.   Or: I'm thinking about you.

This word Dē triggers the ablative, but the ablative and accusative of Tu are both tē, so don't get confused.   And likewise for Ego, the ablative and accusative are both mē as in the next sentence.

Somniāvistī dē mē.   You dreamed of me.

Can you see the connection to insomnia?   Although insomnia means an inability to sleep, Somniāre means to dream. And do you remember the Latin word meaning "to sleep"?

Dormīre   Try to say now I read a book about a pig.

Librum dē porcō lēgī.

Remember the ablative of second-declension nouns is a long O.

Look at this sentence now:

Minerva pictūram dē vītā in Olympō fōrmāvit.

Did you guess what dē vītā means?   Of life
So this sentence means Minerva formed a picture of life in Olympus.

Can you remember how to say yes in Latin?

Ita est.

If you remember, this literally means It is so. And which word means so?

Ita.   The next sentence will begin to explain Arachne's name.

Ita dea Minerva puellam in arāneam mūtāvit.

So the goddess Minerva changed the girl into a spider.

The word arānea means spider in Latin, but the word arachnid is derived from
her name instead of the Latin word. This story was meant to explain how
spiders acquired their web-spinning ability.

Before we start the story, Try to say recall the words in the sentence, I was
also irate.

Quoque īrāta eram.

If you're female and if you're male:

Quoque īrātus eram.

Okay, we're ready for the story now. But pay attention to the different tenses
used and try to figure out why the imperfect is sometimes used and why the
perfect tense is used.

Arachnē et Minerva bene labōrābant. Minerva pictūram pulchram dē vītā in
Olympō fōrmāvit. Deinde Arachnē quoque pictūram pulchram fōrmāvit. Et
Minerva īrāta erat, quod pictūra perfecta erat.
Ita dea Minerva puellam in arāneam mūtāvit.

Arachne and Minerva were working well. Minerva fashioned a beautiful picture of life in Olympus. Then Arachne also formed a beautiful picture. And Minera was irate, because the picture was perfect. So the goddess Minerva changed the girl into a spider.
And the moral of the story is: don't anger the gods.

So did you figure out that in the first sentence, the imperfect was used because it wasn't referring to a completed action: the time was vague. Then we have two sentences in which the action is completed and the perfect is used. Following this, we have two phrases with erat. This is technically the imperfect tense, but it is used for descriptions. The first describes Minerva's state of mind and the second describes the picture. And the last sentence refers to another completed action with the perfect tense.

Okay, we'll play around a little more with iste and ista in the next lesson.

LESSON 22

Today we'll start with a really cool phrase from Sir Thomas Malory's Le Morte d'Arthur:

Yet some men say in many parts of England that King Arthur is not dead, but... many men say that there is written upon his tomb this verse:

Hīc jacet Arthurus, Rex quondam, Rexque futurus.

Here lies Arthur, the once and future king.

Let's break this down. Note first that Rex means King. You can remember this because the T. Rex was unarguably the king of the dinosaurs. But in the second instance it says Rexque. This QUE is another way to say AND, just like ET. Usually it is used for two nouns that are logically linked, but sometimes it is used just to avoid repetition with too many ETs.

This is what makes The once and future king such a good translation. Obviously futurus means future and then quondam means formerly or at one time. So transliterated, this would be The former king and the future king, but the former translation captures the impact of the statement better.

Then we have the word Jacet, which is contained in the word adjacent. One of the meanings of the word Jacet is "is lying prostrate" And note that words that begin with I can also be written with J and vice versa as we'll see in a moment.

But first as a side note, the word Tyrannosaurus in T-Rex didn't fully come from Latin, but the word tyrannis is in fact a Latin word, contained in the following cool saying:

sīc semper tyrannis

This means "thus always to tyrants" implying that bad outcomes will eventually befall tyrants.

Now Sir Thomas Malory said the opening verse was written on Arthur's tomb, but in 1191 some monks in Glastonbury, England claimed to have found the tomb of Arthur and this cross, which is a nightmare to read.

The inscription says:

Hīc iacet sepultus inclitus Rex Arturius in īnsulā Avalōnia.

Here lies buried the famous King Arthur on the Isle of Avalon.

The word Sepultus means buried. This gave us the word sepulchral in English, meaning, related to a tomb. This looks like an adjective but is actually a participle, which are really weird words that lie somewhere between verbs, adjectives, and adverbs. Here it is functioning like a compound verb form. So just think of iacet sepultus as a compound verb meaning "lies buried"

Inclitus is actually an adjective simply meaning famous. If you can think of a good way to remember this word, leave a comment below. And notice that iacet is spelled with an I in this inscription. This is because the J wasn't introduced to Latin until around the time of the Renaissance and Le Morte d'Arthur was written after this.

So since classical Latin used the I, this lesson's story will also use the I, as in the following:

Iūppiter erat rex deōrum et in monte Olympō habitābat. Iūno erat uxor Iovis et rēgīna deōrum. Iūppiter erat deus caelī et Iūno erat dea mātrimōniī.

In the first sentence we have this strange form deōrum, but you probably guessed that this means Of the gods. This is the plural genitive or possessive form for second-declension nouns. And this can help us decode the abbreviation INRI, which you may have seen in paintings of the crucifixion. This stands for:

Iēsūs Nazarēnus, Rex Iūdaeōrum

Nazarēnus is an adjective, so this really means, Nazarene Jesus, King of the Jews, but the first part often gets translated as Jesus of Nazareth. But here we see the -ōrum ending once again. So either of these combinations is a good chunk to learn in order to remember this ending. Let's return to the story now. The second half of the first sentence means lived in mount olympus.

Monte and Olympō are both in the ablative form because they are talking about the location of the living.

Then in the second sentence, we see uxor Iovis. Uxor means wife and Iovis is the possessive form of Iūppiter. Only the nominative form of this name uses Iūppiter, the rest use the stem Iov-. And if you watched the video on the days of the week, you know that Thursday is...

diēs Iovis   Jove's or Jupiter's day

So uxor Iovis means Jupiter's wife. And can you guess what rēgīna deōrum means? Queen of the gods

And the last sentence means Jupiter was god of the sky and Juno was the goddess of marriage. The next section is:

Neptūnus erat frāter Iovis et mare rēgnābat. Et Polyphēmus, Neptūnī fīlius, unum oculum in fronte habēbat.

Here mare is the root of marine and other related words, so this means sea. And rēgnābat means reigned. Can you see the connection between all these words? Rex, rēgīna, rēgnābat all have something to do with reigning. So this first sentence means, Neptune was Jupiter's brother and reigned the sea.

In the next sentence, Polyphemus is the name of the cyclops whom Odysseus met in the Odyssey and in other tales. And here you can probably guess that Neptūnī fīlius means, Neptune's son, or the son of Neptune. And as the name cyclops gives away, he had unum oculum in fronte, or one eye in the forehead. Oculus is one of my favorite words in Latin, and we actually use it in English for the circular openings in domes and as the root in the word ocular. And fronte can mean both front and forehead among many other meanings. So this sentence is, And Polyphemus, the son of Neptune, had one eye in his forehead.

And the final sentences feature a familiar character.

Minerva erat fīlia Iovis sed mātrem nōn habēbat! Minerva ē capite Iovis saluit!

The first sentence should be pretty easy. Minerva was Jupiter's daughter but had no mother! And in the second sentence we have capite, which the word decapitate can help you remember. So ē capite Iovis means out of the head of Jupiter. And saluit is the past tense of salit, which we saw once before. If you remember we used assault to remember that this means jump as in to jump someone. So Minerva jumped out of Jupiter's head. That's the actual Greek myth!

LESSON 23
DIALOGUE 1

In this lesson and the next four lessons, we'll explore a dialogue. These dialogues will use some words from the Lessons, so it is advised that you tackle those also, because repetition is the key to learning a language. This first dialogue will be a simple introduction of a boy and a girl, with a little twist at the end. The girl begins with:

"Salvē, ut valēs?"
"Bene valeō, gratias. Et ut valēs tū?"
"Nōn male."

If you remember, the te on Salvēte makes it plural, so Salvē is what we say when we're speaking to only one person. And this can mean both Hello and Farewell, so it's like aloha.

Then we have ut valēs, which is one of the ways to ask, How are you? In Latin. Here Ut means how and valēs means you are well, or healthy. To me it seems like asking, how do you value? Sort of like how fare you? Try to ask now, how is your father?

Ut pater tuus valet?

It's as easy as that, we can just slip in the person we want to ask about between ut and valet. And can you remember who THIS refers to?

Ut uxor tua valet?   How is your wife?

And one way to answer this question in Latin is:

Bene valeō, gratias.   I am well, thank you.

The other answer in the dialogue was Nōn male.
We have seen the words malus and mala before, but those were adjectives. Male is the adverb form of this word. So the last line means, Not badly. One problem with learning a foreign language is when our own language uses quote incorrect grammar.

In answer to the question how are you, we say I am well. Which is the adverb form of good. But when we answer in the reverse, we say Not bad instead of not badly. Some other ways to answer this question are (in order from good to bad):

optimē – excellently, very well
bene - good
satis bene – okay
male - badly
pessimē – very badly

If you remember, we learned that satis means enough, when you are satisfied, you have had enough. So this is like saying, Good enough Pessimē is the superlative degree or highest degree of male. And obviously this is where the word pessimism comes from, because pessimists always think the worst will happen. Now, optimē, bene, male, and pessimē are all adverbs. Can you give the male and female adjective version of each word?

Optimus optima
bonus bona
malus mala
pessimus pessima

Did you notice something about all these words? For all but bonus, the adverb is formed by adding ē to the stem of each adjective. This is like adding the -ly ending to adjectives in English to form an adverb. Bonus and malus are somewhat irregular just like in English. And just like in English not all adjectives can be converted into an adverb in this way. Let's move on to the next section now.

"Nōmen mihi est Maximus. Quid est nōmen tibi?"
"Nōmen mihi est Alba. Tē nōscēre gaudeō."

This is the most common way to say my name and your name. Mihi and tibi are the dative forms of me and te respectively. So this is like saying, Name to me or Name for me. And remember Quid is contained in the phrase

Quid prō quō

What for what

And Quō is which case? It's the ablative form of Quid

And Quid is the neutral form because nōmen is neutral. The last sentence is a little more difficult.   Gaudeō means I am glad, or I take pleasure in. Gaud kind of looks like glad. So what does this mean?

Gaudeō quod vēnī.

I'm glad I came.   Literally: I'm glad because I came.

The word nōscēre is contained in the words gnostic and agnostic, so this has to do with knowledge. If you squint, you can also kind of see this at the end of the word recognize. And remembering that Tē is both the nominative and accusative form, what do you think this last phrase means?

Literally it is, I'm glad to know you. Or, Nice to meet you. And here's the last section of the dialogue.

"Tū es amīca sorōris meae!"
"Sum. Ut valet soror tuus?"
"Optimē valet, gratias. Salvē."
"Valē."

Sorōris is the genitive or possessive form of soror, which is a third-declension noun. And meae is also a genitive form, but this modifies sorōris, meaning my sister's (with an apostrophe). So this first sentence means You are my sister's friend.

Alba simply answers Sum. This of course means, I am. But it can also fill in for Yes.

Valē is another way to say goodbye. It is the imperative form of valeō, so this is like saying, Be well!

LESSON 24
DIALOGUE 2

Several studies have shown that attempting to guess the meaning of words even when you have no clue can help you acquire these words more strongly than if you didn't try to guess. So in this lesson, we'll go through the dialogue once before explaining each sentence and you should try and guess what the two people are saying. And a hint for one of the words is that this dialogue takes place in the morning. Let's go!

Salvē!
Bonum māne!
Loquorisne latīne?
Tardē loquere, quaesō.
Potesne latīne loquī?
Paululum loquor.
Bene latīne loquoris.
Grātiās!

Bonum māne!

Did you guess that, "Loquorisne latīne?" means "Do you speak Latin?" This is the root of words like loquacious and colloquial and soliloquy.
But this word meaning "to speak" and "to talk" in Latin is strange: the infinitive is loquī and the first-person conjugation is Loquor as you can see in the following table.

Inf. loquī

Ego loquor
Tū   loquoris
(It) loquitur

Imp. loquere

So now can you guess what "Tardē loquere, quaesō." means? Tardē sounds a lot like tardy, right? This means, "Speak slowly, please." Remember, quaesō literally means "I beg" or "I seek" but is the way to say please in Latin. If you know that the Spanish for cheese is queso, it might help to think, Cheese please, queso quaesō. Hahaha

Now, from the last dialogue, we know that Tardē is what type of word? An adverb. So the adjective form would be?

Tarda Tardus   Tardum

And this can also mean late, just like the word tardy, so say now, "You are late."

Tarda es.   If you're talking to a female. And:
Tardus es.   If you're talking to a male.

And instead of just repeating her question verbatim, Alba asks this time, "Potesne latīne loquī?" meaning, "Can you speak Latin?" Remember, when we use Potes, the other verb remains in its infinitive form, which for "speak" is this weird form loquī.

Then we have "Paululum loquor", so this means "I speak (something)"
Paululus is the diminutive form of paulus. Diminutives make things seem smaller or cuter. One such suffix in English is adding a Y-sound. For example, John to Johnny and Dog to Doggy. So since paulus means little or small, paululus means really little. There isn't a direct equivalent to this word in English, but it looks somewhat like paucity, which means scarcity. This is a very common way to say, "just a little." So "Paululum loquor" means, "I speak just a little."
Can you think of how to say, "Give me just a little"?

Da mihi paululum.

Let's use this word for speak a little more.

Cotīdiē cum mātre loquor.   I speak with my mother everyday.

We saw this word cotīdiē in Pater Noster and it is like saying "daily quota". And notice, māter changes to mātre in the ablative form. Remember, cum triggers the ablative. But look at the next sentence.

Tēcum loquor!   I'm talking to you!

Do you see? This first word is the words cum and tē combined into one word, but there is no consensus as to why the order was reversed. And there are other similar combinations like:

nōbīscum   mēcum

These are good words to learn because they tell you the ablative form of these pronouns.

Now, some helpful words to know along with the verb loquī are the names of languages. Can you guess what this sentence means?

Bene hispānice loquoris.   You speak Spanish well.

Do you recognize the form of this word hispānice? It's the vocative form! The vocative form is the same as the nominative form for all but words that end in "-us". But hispānicus is an adjective! This "-icus" suffix is the same as the "-ic" suffix in English and it changes Hispānia, or Spain and Portugal, into the word "Spanish." So to name the language someone speaks, we change the country name into an adjective and decline it in vocative form. It seems complicated, but it also helps us tell the difference between the two uses of the word Spanish. As in Spanish food and I speak Spanish. So that means that latīne is the vocative form of....latīnus. The next language is easy.

Germānice cum patre loquitur.

He or she speaks German with his or her father.

Now you can see that Latin is to blame for why we say German instead of something closer to Deutsch.

The next one might be a little harder.

Paululum gallice loquor.

I speak a little French. During the time of the Roman Empire, the region encompassing France, Belgium, and a few other countries was known as Gaul.

And try to guess now how to say, I speak English.
And remember, during the time of Classical Latin, the English were known as the Angles.

Anglice loquor.   And try to guess this final language name.

Sinice legere potest.   He or she can read Chinese.

You may have seen "Sino-American relations" or "Sino-tibetan languages" referring to China.

Ok, now that we've learned all the words from the dialogue, let's go through it one more time:

Salvē!
Bonum māne!
Loquorisne latīnē?
Tardē loquere, quaesō.
Potesne latīnē loquī?
Paululum loquor.
Bene latīnē loquoris.
Grātiās!

LESSON 25
DIALOGUE 3

As I mentioned in the last dialogue, it is beneficial to try and guess the meaning of words even when you have no clue since this can help you acquire these words more strongly than if you didn't try to guess. So we'll go through the full dialogue again before explaining the new words.

Salvē! Quid agis? Nōmen mihi est Augustus et ē Galliā oriundus sum.
Vīgintī quattor annōs nātus sum et ūna uxor habeō.
Medicīnam in ūniversitāte didicī et nunc medicus sum.

Quid es nōmen tibi? Habēsne frātrēs vel sorōrēs? Quot annōs nātus es?

The first phrase that hasn't been covered is, Quid agis? This means, How's it going? Or: How are you doing? Literally "quid" means "what" and "agis" means "you are doing" We've briefly seen this word agō one or two times. It looks similar to "act" and also means "do", "make", and many other actions. Agis is the tū form of agō and quid is the neutral form of quis.

And we covered how to say, "My name is so and so" in the first dialogue and in your own self-introduction you can of course substitute your own name. Then we have a new construction in the second half of this sentence.

Ē Galliā oriundus sum.   I am from France.

We can use "oriundus" when we want to talk about what country or city, etc. we are from. Oriundus is an adjective meaning something like "originated." So as you can guess, if you're female, you use "oriunda." And we also use the preposition ē, which means "out of" or "from" and as you may have guessed by the long A on Galliā, this preposition triggers the ablative case. So this phrase has a meaning like, "I am originated, out of France." But in English we would say, I am from France.
Let's try some other examples:

Ex Aegyptō oriunda est.   She is from Egypt.

Note here that we used EX instead of Ē. When the following word begins with a vowel or H, we have to use EX. It's like how we use An instead of A before a vowel in English. However, when the next word begins with a consonant, you can use either EX or Ē. Looking at the name for France and recalling that it's Italia, try to guess how to say, "I am from Germany."

Ē Germāniā oriundus sum.

In Latin, many country names end in IA, which makes them first-declension feminine nouns and much easier to conjugate. If you'd like to know other country names, leave a comment below, otherwise we'll move on to the next phrase.

Vīgintī quattor annōs nātus sum.

If you speak a Romance language, you probably guessed what this number was. Vīgintī quattor means twenty four. The important part of this sentence though is the second half. Did you guess that annōs means years? This is the accusative plural of "annus," which we can see is related to "annual". Now here comes the weird part. Nātus is technically a participle. But in English, participles are just past tense verbs that are used as adjectives. For example, cooked, as in cooked food, and boiled as in boiled water. But in Latin, there's more going on. Nātus is like a hidden verb with annōs as its object. And this word gave us the words "prenatal" and "nation".

Remembering the last construction, try to say now, "She is three years old."

Trēs annōs nāta est.

And in the last sentence that Augustus says before asking his questions, he uses the verb didicī. This is hard to recognize, but it's the perfect past tense of discō. Hopefully you remember this word from the very first proverb in the Lessons and can figure out the first half of the sentence.

Medicīnam in ūniversitāte didicī.

So really this means, I learned Medicine in University, but it's the way of saying, I studied blah blah blah in University. And of course, what you studied is in the accusative form. The form of ūniversitāte is harder to recognize because it's a third-declension noun, but this is the ablative form as you may have guessed. Hopefully you can guess this next sentence.

Historiam in ūniversitāte discit.   He is studying history in University.

And Augustus ended his sentence with:

nunc medicus sum.   Now I'm a doctor.

Since this sentence pattern is so easy, I'll just list some other professions:

Vigil   Someone who is vigilant can be a watchman, guard, or police.

Vēnditor   Sounds a lot like vendor. This is a seller. And a obvious one is:

Architectus

Now, the Romans obviously didn't have as many job titles as we now have, since they didn't even have computers. But some of these titles have been added to New Latin, although there isn't always consensus on some of these terms.

And Augustus asked a few questions at the end.

The first we saw in the first dialogue. And the second was:

Habēsne frātrēs vel sorōrēs?

Note that "frāter" loses the E and becomes "frātr-" in the plural. So it's frātrēs and not *frāterēs. What do you think this word "vel" means? It means, "or", right? And it can mean both.

And finally, the way to ask someone's age is:

Quot annōs nātus es?

Quot means how many. So how would we ask, How many brothers do you have?

Quot frātrēs habēs?

And now let's go through the dialogue one more time.

Salvē! Quid agis? Nōmen mihi est Augustus et ē Galliā oriundus sum.

Vīgintī quattor annōs nātus sum et ūna uxor habeō.
Medicīnam in ūniversitāte didicī et nunc medicus sum.

Quid es nōmen tibi? Habēsne frātrēs vel sorōrēs? Quot annōs nātus es?

LESSON 26
DIALOGUE 4

In this lesson we will focus on the word for "to go" because it's partially irregular in Latin just like in English. We'll start out with a short dialogue and try and guess which word means "go" in the first four sentences.

Quō īs?
Eō domum. Et quō īs tū?
Ad tabernam eō. Flōrēs emere volō.
Taberna clausa est.
Malum! Nunc domum eō.

Et domōs eunt.

We saw three different forms of the verb meaning "to go"

Eō   I go
īs   you go
eunt   they go

So you can probably guess that,

Quō īs?   Means "Where are you going?" Remember, most of the Wh-question words begin with Qu in Latin. And the infinitive of "to go" is īre, so īs is a regular conjugation. Then we had:

Eō domum.   I am going home.

If you're above a certain age, you can remember this by thinking, Captain Eō had a cool way of going. i.e. moonwalking, because he was Michael Jackson.

Then one person asks, And we are you going, to which the other person replies:

Ad tabernam eō.   I am going to the store.

Remember, the preposition "ad" triggers the accusative. Taberna can mean shop or store and also inn or tavern, which is where this word comes from.

The next sentence contains an easy word to guess and one that's hard to guess.

Flōrēs emere volō.   I want to buy flowers.

Flōrēs is easy, right? But emere is harder to connect to an English word. However, it's found at the end of the word "redeem" and perhaps you can remember this word by thinking, I'll redeem a coupon in order to buy this. Then we have:

Taberna clausa est.   Followed by,   Malum!

Can you guess what this means?   The store is closed. Darn!

And the last sentence contains words we know but in different forms:

Et domōs eunt.

Here domōs is the plural accusative form of domus and eunt is the plural form of eō, so it means they go. And notice, domōs has no preposition, but the accusative form is used to indicate the object or goal of the movement.

Let's use this verb īre a little more. If "you go" is īs, can you guess what "she goes" is?

it   For example:

Ad scholam it per pedēs.   He or she goes to school by foot.

The connection between pedēs and pedestrian is pretty obvious. But pedēs is the plural form, so per pedēs is more like saying, "by feet". Which makes more sense since we're not hopping. Try to guess now how to say, "We go."

īmus   The we form is the most regular. Here's an example using this word.

Sōlis diēbus in ecclēsiam īmus.   We go to church on Sundays.

You have probably heard of Ecclesiastical Latin, which is also sometimes called Church Latin. Ecclēsia simply means church. And the phrase Sōlis diēbus is a good chunk to learn, because it contains the plural ablative form. That makes sense, doesn't it? We use the ablative to indicate at what place in time the event occurs and it's plural because it's every Sunday. Let's try another sentence like this. Remembering that Monday is Moonday, try to say, I go to the store on Mondays.

Lūnae diēbus ad tabernam eō.

One thing I've skipped over until now, because I didn't want to make the conjugation so overwhelming, is that there is a plural "you" form. So, "you guys go", is:

Ītis   And try to say, You guys are going to the forest.

Ad silvam ītis.

This ending "-tis" is the "you plural" conjugation. But for regular verbs, we just add "-ti" before the "s" in the You-conjugation. So īs becomes ītis. It's a little like adding TE to "salvē" to make it plural. So how would we say, "You guys love"?

Amātis   And, "You guys have one brother"?

Ūnum fratrem habētis.

We're going to revisit the dialogue again now, but this time in the past tense.

Quō īvistī?
Īvī domum. Et quō īvistī tū?
Ad tabernam īvī. Flōrēs emere volēbam, sed taberna clausa erat.
Malum!

This contained the forms īvī and īvistī. Try to say now, I went by foot.

Per pedēs īvī.   And now, "Did you go to school"?

Īvistīne ad scholam?

As you can see, this verb isn't so irregular and it's pretty easy to conjugate since it's usually just "ī" plus the appropriate ending. In the conjugations we've just seen, the irregular forms were

eō and eunt

so these are the only forms you have to memorize. Good luck!

Ego	eō
Tū	īs
(it)	it
Nōs	īmus
Vōs	ītis
(they)	eunt

LESSON 27
DIALOGUE 5

In this dialogue, we will learn the perfect past tense of "sum" or "to be." It is technically "irregular", because it is different from the present tense, but in reality it is just FU plus the regular perfect past tense endings. For example, the dialogue will begin with:

fuī
fuistī
fui
fuimus
fuistis
fuērunt

Fuistīne umquam

So what does this first word mean? Were you. This is the past tense of the Tu conjugation for "es". And this second word, umquam, means "ever" or "at any time." So this is the way to say, "Have you ever been..." But we will also see the imperfect past tense form in the dialogue, so hopefully you can remember it.

And there is one word that will look familiar, but has a slightly different meaning than what you might guess.

Negōtiōsus

If you're constantly negotiating, then you're doing a lot of business. This word simply means busy.

Okay, you should be able to guess much of the rest of the dialogue, so we'll begin it now.

Fuistīne umquam in Āfricā?
Numquam ibī fuī.
Cūr nōn?
Negōtiōsa eram.
Intellegō.
Sed frāter meus in Āfricā fuit.
Quotiēs ibī fuit?
Ibī fuit quīnquiēs.
Quam mīrābilis!

From what was said in the introduction, I'm sure you understood that the first sentence means, Have you ever been to Africa? Then Valentina replies,

Numquam ibī fuī.

As you may have guessed, since umquam means "ever", numquam means "never". And this other word, ibī, just means "there" or "in that place". So say now, A poet lives there.

Poēta ibī habitat.   And ask, Is there water there?

Estne aqua ibī?

Then the boy asks, "Why not?"   Cūr nōn?

Cūr is one of the Wh-question words that does not begin with QU, but C is close in sound. And maybe you can remember it by the association, Someone who is always asking why is a cur. Remembering that a fugitive runs away, try to ask, Why did you run away?

Cūr fūgistī?

That was sort of a trick question because in the perfect past the U lengthens. So how would we say, Why are you running away?

Cūr fugis?

Valentina answers with

Negōtiōsa eram.   Which as I said in the intro, means I was busy.

But do you understand why she used eram instead of fuī? Because it was an unspecified or incomplete span of time. Now if we were going to say, I was busy yesterday, or

hesternō diē   how would we say this?

Hesternō diē negōtiōsus fuī.

And do you see the connection between yesterday and Hesternō diē? Yester
Hester Day diē The only problem is that because this is Latin, we have to
decline the nouns. And as you might have guessed, Hesternō diē is the
ablative form of each word, because it's indicating at what place in time the
action occurred. The boy replies:

Intelligō.

This is the way of saying, "I understand" or "I get it". Like saying, it is
intelligible. Use this now to say, I don't understand you.

Tē nōn intelligō.

We have to use the accusative form of Tu, which is Tē. And try to say now,
he or she understands Latin.

Linguam Latīnum intelligit.

Then Valentina adds that her brother has been to Africa, to which the boy
asks,

Quotiēs ibī fuit?

And Valentina answers, He has been there five times. Or:

Ibī fuit quīnquiēs.

In these two sentences the suffix "-iēs" is attached to the words quotiēs and
quīnque, giving the meaning of "number of times". So quotiēs means how
many times and quīnquiēs means five times. We can attach this suffix to
many nouns, although sometimes the end of the word must change. Can you
remember what the following sentence means?

Quotiēs in diē edis?   How many times do you eat in a day.

And the boy ends the dialogue with,

Quam mīrābilis!
To me mīrābilis sounds like a combination of miracle and marvelous. And indeed it means both miraculous and marvelous. And Quam means how, so this means, How marvelous!

Ok, let's go through the dialogue one more time.

Fuistīne umquam in Āfricā?
Numquam ibī fuī.
Cūr nōn?
Negōtiōsa eram.
Intellegō.
Sed frāter meus in Āfricā fuit.
Quotiēs ibī fuit?
Ibī fuit quīnquiēs.
Quam mīrābilis!

LESSON 28

In this lesson we'll learn some Latin and a little bit about Roman homes, or the domus. This story's lesson will be a description of the traditional home in Ancient Rome.

This lesson's story begins with the sentence:

Ecce domus rōmāna.

The word Ecce is used to call attention to something, so it's like saying, "Behold" or "Look at..." And domus rōmāna means Roman house. Remember, domus is weird, because it looks like a second-declension noun, but is feminine, so the adjective rōmāna is in feminine form. And domus actually declines with a mixture of second-declension and fourth-declension endings as we can see in the next sentence.

Domus in urbe erat et taberna ante domum erat.

If you remember, taberna means store. As you can see in the picture, many Roman homes had a store "ante domum" or in the front of the house. When ante is used as a preposition, it triggers the accusative. Another preposition that triggers the accusative is "iūxtā" or next to, as in:

Taberna iūxtā ōstium erat.

The store was next to the door or entrance.

Remember, when you juxtapose two things, you place one thing iūxtā the other.

And we actually have the word ostium in English, but it's probably only familiar to people who studied anatomy. Instead, you can remember this by thinking, I ostracized him by shutting the ōstium on him. And what declension and gender is this noun? Second-declension neutral. Like vīnum. The plural form is in the next sentence:

In domus erant duo ōstia.   In the house there were two doors.

And neutral nouns have the same nominative and accusative forms for both plural and singular as in the next sentences:

Dominus per ōstium magnum intrābat. Servī per ōstium parvum intrābant.

The master used to enter through the large door. The servants used to enter through the small door.

These are all words we've seen before except per. Latin uses this word more like in the expression, "Send it per express." So it means, "through" or "by means of". And using the perfect past tense, can you think of how to say, He or she walked through the forest?

Per silvam ambulāvit.

For the next sentence, try to guess what the new word means:

Dominus dīves in magnō domō cum multīs servīs habitābat.

The rich master lived in a large house with many slaves.

I think this is the first third-declension adjective we've seen. But it can also be used on its own as a noun to mean "rich man", which means that sometimes it can be ambiguous as in:

Dīves es, quod dīligenter labōrābās.

You are rich because you worked hard.   Or the first half could also mean, you are a rich man.

And maybe you can remember this by thinking, a rich man Dīves can work on his dives because he owns a pool.

Note also that in the original sentence

magnō domō and multīs servīs

are the singular and plural forms of the ablative case. Now we have more description of the house:

In domus rōmāna magnum ātrium cum impluviō erat. Pluvia in impluvium cadēbat.

Ātrium has the same meaning as atrium in English, an entrance hall, but as you can see from the picture it looks a little different than what you might be used to. This is because in the center of the room they had an impluvium which was used to catch rain, or pluvia. This was then filtered through layers of sand and gravel and served as a naturally cooled water-supply.

And maybe you can associate pluvia with puddles or plumage raining down. The other new word in the second sentence was cadēbat or cadere. This has many connections to English words, so you can take your pick between cadaver, cascade, decadent...whichever helps you remember this word. The following example sentence is practically English:

Autumnō folia cadunt.   Leaves or foliage fall in Autumn.

Then we have:

In ātriō nūllae fenestrae erat, quod iūxtā ātrium multa cubicula erant.

Before, we saw that the plural of ōstium was ōstia and here we see the plural of cubiculum. This is where English got the word cubicle. And the word cubāre means to lie down, so this was the word for a small bedroom. The other word we don't know is fenestra, which means window. So this sentence means,

In the atrium there were no windows, because next to the atrium there were bedchambers.

This story is good practice for the ablative case, because the next sentence also contains the singular and plural ablative forms of cubiculum.

In cubiculīs familia et servī dormiēbant, sed multī servī in ūnō cubiculō parvō dormiēbant.

The family and servants slept in the bedchambers, but many servants used to sleep in one bedchamber.

Nota bene: All the sentences were in the imperfect past tense for two reasons: erat and its derivatives were used because they were descriptions and the rest were used because they were describing what USED to be done. They used to enter, they used to live, they used to sleep, rain used to fall. Keep this in mind as we go through the story in full now.

Domus

Ecce domus rōmāna. Domus in urbe erat et taberna ante domum erat.
Taberna iūxtā ōstium erat. In domus erant duo ōstia: ōstium magnum et
ōstium parvum. Dominus et familia per ōstium magnum intrābant. Servī et
ancillae per ōstium parvum intrābant. Dominus dīves in magnō domō cum
multīs servīs habitābat. In domus rōmāna magnum ātrium cum impluviō erat.
Pluvia in impluvium cadēbat. In ātriō nūllae fenestrae erat, quod iūxtā atrium
multa cubicula erant. In cubiculīs familia et servī dormiēbant, sed multī servī
in ūnō cubiculō parvō dormiēbant.

The Roman house

Behold the Roman house. The house is in the city and there is a store in front
of the house. The store is next to the entrance. In the house there were two
doors: the large door and the small door. The master and his family used to
enter through the large door. The servants and maids used to enter through
the small door. The rich masters used to live in a large house with many
servants. In the Roman house, there used to be a large atrium with an
impluvium. Rain used to fall in the impluvium. There used to be no windows
in the atrium, because there used to be bedchambers next to the atrium. The
family and servants used to sleep in the bedchambers, but many servants used
to sleep in one small bedchamber..

LESSON 29

In this lesson, we're going to revisit the passive tense. We explored this tense a little in the lesson on Pater Noster, but we'll go into more depth here.

First of all, let's figure out exactly what the passive tense is. Look at the next two sentences.

I pick up the apple. The apple is picked up by me.

They describe the exact same action. But in the first sentence, the subject, I, is actively doing the action. And in the second sentence, the subject is "the apple" and the action is being done to it. The one doing the action, me, is just added on the end and isn't even needed. In passive sentences, we can just say,

The apple is picked up. Without any mention of who or what actually did the action.

And notice, the passive form in English is kind of weird. We add is, and put the verb in the past tense. So "pick up" becomes "is picked up". Latin uses conjugation as you might expect. Let's look at how the following sentence changes.

Servus aquam portat. The slave carries water.

Aqua portātur. The water is carried.

The verb portat gets it's last vowel lengthened and the ending UR added to it, making it portātur.
Notice, not only did the verb change, but aquam changed to aqua, because as we saw earlier, the object becomes the subject and Latin reflects this change, much more obviously than English does. And if we want to add "by the slave", we use the following construction:

Aqua ā servō portātur. The water is carried by the slave.

As you may have guessed, the noun following ā is declined in the ablative case. Try a sentence for yourself now. Change the following sentence into the passive form.

Puella puerum videt.   The girl sees the boy.

Puer ā puellā vidētur.   The boy is seen by the girl.

In the next sentence, try to guess the new word.

Liber ā puerō capitur.   The book is picked up by the boy.

Do you see the connection between capitur and capture? That's where this English word came from. And in Latin it can also mean to take, or hold. Can you guess what this sentence would be in active form?

Puer librum capit.

Can you figure out what the next sentence means?

Ab omnibus amātur.   He or she is loved by everyone.
Omnibus is the plural ablative form of omnis, whose plural form is omnēs as we know from the beginning of each book. This is a third-declension noun. Note also that when the following word begins with a vowel sound, ā changes to ab. However, ab can be used at any time.

Here's another third-declension noun.

Ā parentibus amor.   I am loved by my parents.

For first-person, the O gets shortened and just an R is added, so this is sort of the opposite of the third-person case. The only problem is that there is no pattern for when the vowel is shortened or lengthened, but it is more important that we can understand this form when we read, than know every conjugation exactly. And as you can see in this chart, many of the endings end in UR.

There are some words that don't have a passive form because it doesn't really make sense to put them in passive form. For example, Dormiō does not have a passive form, because saying He is sleeped makes no sense. And some words like labōrō only have a third-person passive form.

But if you're like me, you were probably told throughout your schooling to never use the passive form, to always convert sentences into active form. So why do we need to learn this form? Because it actually has a lot of use and power. We can describe an action without stating who performed it. And in this way, we can put emphasis on the recipient of the action. Thus many great lines from literature are written in the passive, like the following:

Nihil sine labōre mortālibus datur.   Nothing is given to mortals without effort.

Here Nothing is emphasized much more than if we said, "They give nothing to mortals without effort."
The word sans in English, meaning without, came from French, but was derived from this word "sine".
For the next sentence, if you recall, we learned that ducere means to lead, like an air duct:

Nōn dūcor, dūcō.   I am not lead, I lead.   And what do you think this means?

Dē tē fābula nārrātur.   Of yourself the tale is told.

Remember, this word Dē is what eventually replaced the genitive form in Vulgar Latin, so here it means, "of". And fābula is where the word fable came from, so the end is like saying, "the fable is narrated". Next we have:

Arbor ā frūctibus cognōscitur.   A tree is known by its fruit.

The Latin word for fruit is frūctus. Nice, huh? And the word recognōscō means recognize, so, recalling that RE means again, cognōscō means come to know or learn.

And let's end with an irregular verb. The verb faciō, meaning to do or make, loses the AC in the passive form and is in the next sentence:

Ex nihilō nihil fit.   Nothing is made from nothing.

Ok, hopefully that wasn't too complicated and that you'll be able to recognize some of the forms, because many great lines and mottos are written in the passive   form   as   we   just   saw.

LESSON 30

In this lesson we're going to practice some more with some third declension nouns. Let's go through the story line by line.

Avēs volant et piscēs natant. Avēs in āere volant. Piscēs in aquā natant.

Birds fly and fish swim. Birds fly in the air. Fish swim in water.

We have either already seen all these words before, or can guess them. But the one word to pay attention to is āere. This is the ablative form of āer, a third declension noun. It is regular in all but it's nominative form, āer, but this is easy to remember since it's so close to its English equivalent, air. The story continues:

Quōmodo haec avis dīcitur?

Quōmodo   What mode? Or, In what way?

And do you recognize dīcitur? This is the passive form of dīcit, which we went through in the last lesson. So altogether this means, "In what way is this bird called?" Or simply, "What is this bird called?" And from the word "haec", we know that avis is what gender? Feminine. That's one big problem with third-declension nouns, because although avis is feminine, piscis is masculine.
And the answer to this question is:

Aquila dīcitur.   It is called an eagle.

Quills were probably made of eagle feathers. This bird name is important to know because it was the standard carried by Roman Legions. Let's continue:

Avēs ālās habent, ergo volāre possunt. Avēs ālīs volant.

Birds have wings, therefore they can fly. Birds fly with their wings.

This is the first time we have seen the ablative form used on its own. It is more frequently used following a preposition, but it can also be used on its own with the meaning of "by means of". I think this is also the first time we have seen a first-declension noun in the plural ablative form. However, first- and second-declension nouns have the same ending, īs. The next sentence contains the plural ablative form of a third-declension noun:

Pedibus ad scholam eō.   I go to school by foot.

So here again the ablative form is used on its own to mean "by means of", so this means "by foot" or "on foot". Next we have:

Aliī piscēs ālās habent, aliī nōn ālās habent.

Here is the plural form of the word "alius," which means other. So this sort of means, "Others fish have wings, others don't have wings." But when aliī is used in a pair like this, it functions more like "some...others"

So it's, "Some fish have wings, others don't have wings."

And at this point it shouldn't be surprising that alius must be declined to match the noun that follows.

Alia tempora, aliī mōrēs.   Other times, other customs.

Here alia is the neutral plural form and aliae would be the female plural version.

Tempora should be pretty clear from its connection with tempo. It simply means a period of time. And we actually have this word mōrēs in English and miraculously it has the same pronunciation and meaning as the Latin word. Here is another example:

Aliī hominēs natāre possunt, aliī nōn possunt.

Hominēs is another third-declension noun and it is which gender? Masculine. And the nominative form is Homō.

Let's play around a little more with third-declension nouns. Try to say, The man looks at the fish.

Homō piscem spectat.

This is the regular conjugation for third-declension nouns. So for the accusative case of first-declension we have AM, for second-declension we have UM, and for third-declension we have EM. And remembering back to the form of Homō we saw earlier, try to say, I see a man.

Hominem videō.   The stem of this word is

Homin-   it is only the nominative case that's irregular. This is common in third-declension nouns as we saw with āēr.

Try to guess the meaning of the following sentence:

Canis amīcus optimus hominis est.   Dog is man's best friend.

The IS ending is the genitive or possessive form. But notice that it matches the Nominative form of some nouns like piscis and avis.

Let's review the cases we've learned so far.

Nominative	piscis		avis	canis	homō		āēr
Genitive	piscis		avis	canis	hominis		āeris
Accusative	piscem		avem	canem	hominem		āerem
Ablative	pisce	ave	cane	homine		āere	

Nominative	piscēs		avēs	canēs	hominēs		āerēs
Accusative	piscēs		avēs	canēs	hominēs		āerēs
Ablative	piscibus	avibus	canibus	hominibus	āeribus		

Just note the patterns, don't try to memorize the chart. The key pattern to note is that the first-declension is characterized by A sounds, the second-declension by U and O sounds, and this declension by I and E sounds.

Ok, let's go through the story now in full.

Avēs et Piscēs

Avēs volant et piscēs natant. Avēs in āere volant. Piscēs in aquā natant.
Quōmodo haec avis dīcitur? Aquila dīcitur. Avēs ālās habent, ergo volāre
possunt. Avēs ālīs volant.

Aliī piscēs ālās habent, aliī piscēs nōn ālās habent. Sed volāre nōn possunt.
Piscēs in aquā vīvunt. Aliī hominēs natāre possunt, aliī nōn possunt.

Birds and Fish

Birds fly and fish swim. Birds fly in the air. Fish swim in water. What is this
bird called? It is called an eagle. Birds have wings, therefore they can fly.
Birds fly with their wings.

Some fish have wings, other fish don't have wings. But they cannot fly. Fish
live   in   water.   Some   humans   can   swim,   others   cannot.."

FULL STORIES

Pān et Syringa

Ōlim erat nympha pulchra, quae nōmen Syringa erat.

Omnēs deī Syringam amābant, sed Syringa deōs nōn amābat. Syringa deōs fugitābat et sē in silvā occultābat.

Deus Pān, quī in silvā habitābat, Syringam vīdit et eam amābat. Pān dīxit, "Tē amō."

Sed nympha misera ad fluvium fugitāvit. Syringa ad nymphās clāmāvit, "Ō nymphae! Fōrmam meam mūtāte!"

Deinde nymphae eam in papȳrōs in fluviō mūtāvit. Pān papȳrōs vīdit et eōs amābat.

Dēnique septem papȳrōs adhaesit et fistulam fōrmāvit.

Pan and Syrinx

Once upon a time, there was a beautiful nymph whose name was Syrinx.

All the gods loved Syrinx, but Syrinx did not love the gods. Syrinx fled from the gods and hid herself in the forest.

The god Pan, who lived in the forest, saw Syrinx and loved her. Pan said, "I love you."

But the miserable nymph fled to the river. Syrinx cried to the nymphs, "Oh nymphs! Change my form!"

Then the nymphs changed her into paper reeds in the river. Pan saw the reeds and loved them.

Finally, he attached seven reeds and formed a fistula.

Videsne fluvius? Nīlus est. Hic fluvius vēlōciter fluit. Multī piscēs in fluviō natant.

Ubi est Nīlus? Nīlus nōn in Eurōpā est. In Āfricā est.

Mississippiensis quoque fluvius est. Sed Mississippiensis nōn in Āfricā est. In Americā est.

Quam longus est fluvius Nīlus? Nīlus est fluvius longissimus mundī.

Rōma urbs antīqua est. Haec urbs in Ītaliā est. Urbs historica est.

Estne Rōma urbs magna? Habitasne in urbē? Bibliothēca in urbē est.

Multī librī in bibliothēcā sunt. Bibliothēca in mediā urbē est. Ubi est schola tua? Schola iūxtā bibliothēcam est.

Rivers and Cities

Do you see the river? It is the Nile. This river flows rapidly. Many fish swim in the river.

Where is the Nile? The Nile is not in Europe. It is in Africa.

The Mississippi is also a river. But the Mississippi is not in Africa. It is in America.

How long is the Nile? The Nile is the world's longest river.

Rome is an ancient city. This city is in Italy. It is a historical city.

Is Rome a large city? Do you live in the city? There is a library in the city.

There are many books in the library. The library is in the middle of the city. Where is your school? The school is next to the library.

Minerva dea erat. Erat dea artium. Arachnē erat puella quoque perīta in artibus.   Arachnē in casā minūtā habitābat et pictūrās pulchrās fōrmāvit. Dum nymphae spectābant, saepe pictūrās in textilī fōrmāvit.

Nymphae pictūrās vīdit et puellam laudāvit. "Quis est magistra tibī? Certē Minerva tibī artem dedit."

Sed Arachnē superba erat et sapientiam nōn habuit. Sē laudāvit et clāmāvit, "Minerva nōn mē docuit. Nēmō mihi magistra est. Mē docuī. Fōrmō pictūrās melius quam Minerva."

Dea Minerva fōrmam fēminae simulāvit et ad terram īvit. Dīxit ad puellam, "Contrītium praecēdit superbia. Certāmus!"

Arachnē et Minerva bene labōrābant. Minerva pictūram pulchram dē vītā in Olympō fōrmāvit. Deinde Arachnē quoque pictūram pulchram fōrmāvit. Et Minerva īrāta erat, quod pictūra perfecta erat.
Ita dea Minerva puellam in arāneam mūtāvit.

Arachne

Minerva was a goddess. She was goddess of the arts. Arachne was a girl also skilled in the arts. Arachne lived in a tiny cottage and formed beautiful pictures. While the nymphs were watching, she often fashioned pictures in textile.

The nymphs looked at the pictures and praised the girl. "Who is your teacher? Certainly Minerva gave you your art."

But Arachne was proud and was not wise (did not have wisdom). She praised herself and cried, "Minerva did not teach me. No one is my teacher. I taught myself. I form pictures better than Minerva."

The goddess Minerva simulated feminine form and went to the earth. She said to the girl, "Pride goeth before a fall. (Contrition precedes pride.) Let's compete!"

Arachne and Minerva were working well. Minerva fashioned a beautiful picture of life in Olympus. Then Arachne also formed a beautiful picture. And Minera was irate, because the picture was perfect. So the goddess Minerva changed the girl into a spider.

Deī

Iūppiter erat rex deōrum et in monte Olympō habitābat. Iūno erat uxor Iovis et rēgīna deōrum. Iūppiter erat deus caelī et Iūno erat dea mātrimōniī.

Neptūnus erat frāter Iovis et mare rēgnābat. Et Polyphēmus, Neptūnī fīlius, unum oculum in fronte habēbat.

Minerva erat fīlia Iovis sed mātrem nōn habēbat! Minerva ē capite Iovis saluit!

The Gods

Jupiter was the king of the gods and lived in Mount Olympus. Juno was Jupiter's wife and queen of the gods. Jupiter was god of the sky and Juno was the goddess of marriage.

Neptune was Jupiter's brother and reigned the sea. And Polyphemus, Neptune's son, had one eye in his forehead.

Minerva was Jupiter's daughter but did not have a mother! Minerva jumped out of Jupiter's head!

"Salvē, ut valēs?"
"Bene valeō, gratias. Et ut valēs tū?"
"Nōn male."
"Tū es amīca sorōris meae!"
"Sum. Ut valet soror tuus?"
"Optimē valet, gratias. Salvē."
"Valē."

"Hello, how are you?"
"I'm fine, thank you. And how are you?"
"Not bad."
"My name is Maximus. What is your name?"
"My name is Alba. Nice to meet you."
"You are my sister's friend!"
"Yes. How is your sister?"
"She is great, thanks. Goodbye."
"Take care."

Salvē!
Bonum māne!
Loquorisne latīnē?
Tardē loquere, quaesō.
Potesne latīnē loquī?
Paululum loquor.
Bene latīnē loquoris.
Grātiās!

Bene hispānice loquoris.
Germānice cum patre loquitur.
Paululum gallice loquor.
Anglice loquor.
Sinice legere potest.

Hello!
Good morning!
Do you speak Latin?
Speak slowly, please.
Can you speak Latin?
I speak a little.
You speak Latin well!
Thanks!

You speak Spanish well.
He or she speaks German with his or her father.
I speak a little French.
I speak English.
He or she can read Chinese.

Salvē! Quid agis?
Nōmen mihi est Augustus et ē Galliā oriundus sum.
Vīgintī quattor annōs nātus sum et ūna uxor habeō.
Medicīnam in ūniversitāte didicī et nunc medicus sum.

Quid es nōmen tibi? Habēsne frātrēs vel sorōrēs? Quot annōs nātus es?

Hello! How are you doing?
My name is Augustus and I am from France.
I'm twenty-four years old and have a wife.
I studied medicine at University and now I'm a doctor.

What is your name? Do you have brothers or sisters? How old are you?

Quō īs?
Eō domum. Et quō īs tū?
Ad tabernam eō. Flōrēs emere volō.
Taberna clausa est.
Malum! Nunc domum eō.

Et domōs eunt.

Quō īvistī?
Īvī domum. Et quō īvistī tū?
Ad tabernam īvī. Flōrēs emere volēbam, sed taberna clausa erat.
Malum!

Where are you going?
I'm going home. And where are you going?
I'm going to the store. I want to buy flowers.
The store is closed.
Darn!

And they go home.

Where did you go?
I went home. And where did you go?
I went to the store. I wanted to buy flowers, but the store was closed.
Darn!

Dialogue 5

Fuistīne umquam in Āfricā?
Numquam ibī fuī.
Cūr nōn?
Negōtiōsa eram.
Intellegō.
Sed frāter meus in Āfricā fuit.
Quotiēs ibī fuit?
Ibī fuit quīnquiēs.
Quam mīrābilis!

Have you ever been to Africa?
I have never been there.
Why not?
I was busy.
I understand.
But my brother has been to Africa.
How many times has he been there?
He has been there five times.
How wonderful!

Domus

Ecce domus rōmāna. Domus in urbe erat et taberna ante domum erat.
Taberna iūxtā ōstium erat. In domus erant duo ōstia: ōstium magnum et
ōstium parvum. Dominus et familia per ōstium magnum intrābant. Servī et
ancillae per ōstium parvum intrābant. Dominus dīves in magnō domō cum
multīs servīs habitābat. In domus rōmāna magnum ātrium cum impluviō erat.
Pluvia in impluvium cadēbat. In ātriō nūllae fenestrae erat, quod iūxtā atrium
multa cubicula erant. In cubiculīs familia et servī dormiēbant, sed multī servī
in ūnō cubiculō parvō dormiēbant.

The Roman House

Behold the Roman house. The house is in the city and there is a store in
front of the house. The store is next to the entrance. In the house there were
two doors: the large door and the small door. The master and his family used
to enter through the large door. The servants and maids used to enter
through the small door. The rich masters used to live in a large house with
many servants. In the Roman house, there used to be a large atrium with an
impluvium. Rain used to fall in the impluvium. There used to be no windows
in the atrium, because there used to be bedchambers next to the atrium. The
family and servants used to sleep in the bedchambers, but many servants used
to sleep in one small bedchamber.

Avēs et Piscēs

Avēs volant et piscēs natant. Avēs in āere volant. Piscēs in aquā natant. Quōmodo haec avis dīcitur? Aquila dīcitur. Avēs ālās habent, ergo volāre possunt. Avēs ālīs volant.

Aliī piscēs ālās habent, aliī piscēs nōn ālās habent. Sed volāre nōn possunt. Piscēs in aquā vīvunt. Aliī hominēs natāre possunt, aliī nōn possunt.

Birds and Fish

Birds fly and fish swim. Birds fly in the air. Fish swim in water. What is this bird called? It is called an eagle. Birds have wings, therefore they can fly. Birds fly with their wings.

Some fish have wings, other fish don't have wings. But they cannot fly. Fish live in water. Some humans can swim, others cannot.

9 798423 052317